KEY STAGE 2
Levels 3–5

Test Paper 1

Maths

Test Paper 1 (calculator **not** allowed)

D1576270

Test Paper 1 (calculator **not** allowed)

Instructions:

- find a quiet place where you can sit down and complete the test paper undisturbed
- make sure you have all the necessary equipment to complete the test paper
- read the questions carefully
- answer all the questions in this booklet
- go through and check your answers when you have finished the test paper

Time:

This test paper is **45 minutes** long.

Note to Parents:

Check how your child has done against the mark scheme in the Instructions, Answers and Mark Scheme Booklet.

Page	3	5	7	9	11	13	14	Max. Mark	**Actual Mark**
Score	....	....	....	....	....	....	....	40	....

First name ....

Last name ....

1 Write the missing numbers in the calculations below.

a) $6.3 \times \boxed{} = 6300$

(1 mark) Q1a

b) $1040 \div 100 = \boxed{}$

(1 mark) Q1b

2 Here is a square divided into identical smaller squares.

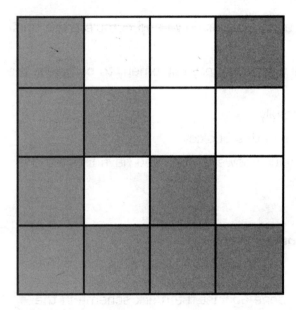

What fraction of the square is not shaded? $\boxed{}$

(1 mark) Q2

3 The toy shop has a sale on, *Buy one and get one free.*

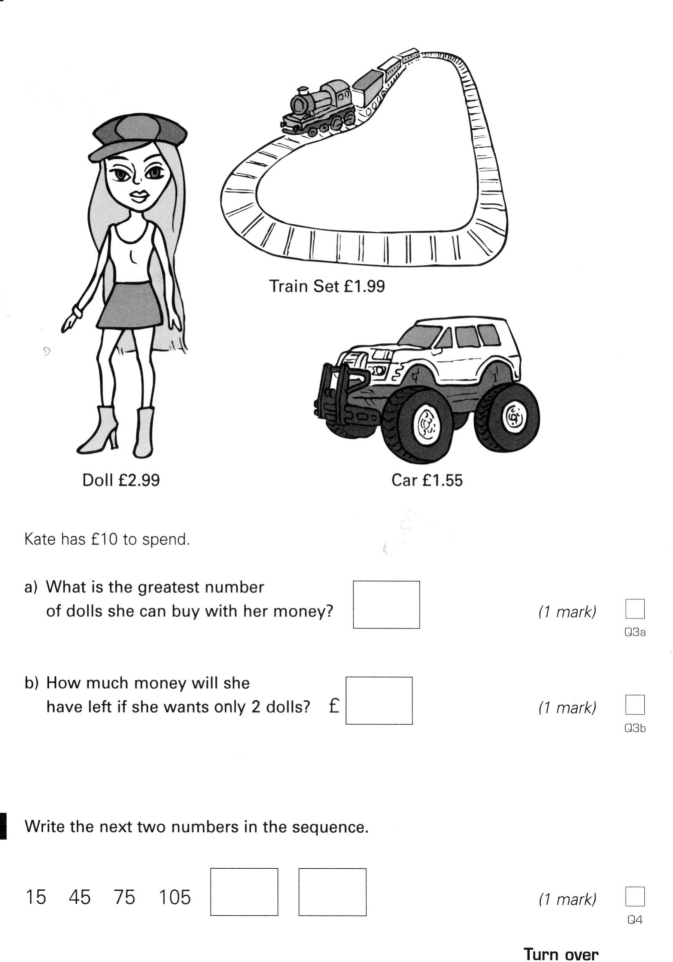

Train Set £1.99

Doll £2.99

Car £1.55

Kate has £10 to spend.

a) What is the greatest number
of dolls she can buy with her money?

(1 mark)
Q3a

b) How much money will she
have left if she wants only 2 dolls? £

(1 mark)
Q3b

4 Write the next two numbers in the sequence.

15   45   75   105

(1 mark)
Q4

Turn over

subtotal

5 This is the time Sally starts her walk to grandma's house.

The walk takes 45 minutes.

What time did Sally arrive at grandma's?

(1 mark)

Q5

6 **Round up these decimals to the nearest whole number.**

27.6 m [ ] m   79.4 km [ ] km   *(1 mark)*

Q6

7 Ben did a survey in school about the children's pets.

He then drew this Venn diagram.

a) **How many children had a dog for a pet?** [ ]   *(1 mark)*

Q7a

b) **Which was the least popular pet?**

Circle the correct answer.   CAT   DOG   FISH   *(1 mark)*

Q7b

8 Measure accurately the longest side of this shape.

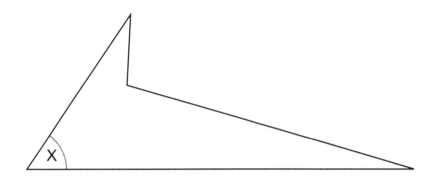

a) Give your answer in millimetres. ☐ mm   *(1 mark)* ☐
                                                                    Q8a

b) Measure the angle x using a protractor. ☐ °   *(1 mark)* ☐
                                                                    Q8b

9 Circle two numbers that add up to make 0.81.

0.24   0.09   0.9   0.51   0.57   0.17   *(1 mark)* ☐
                                                                    Q9

10 Sam weighs some sand. He weighs 225 grams of sand.

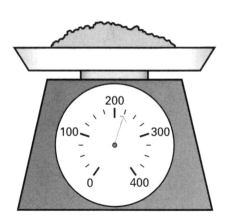

Draw an arrow on the scale to show 225 grams.   *(1 mark)* ☐
                                                                    Q10

Turn over

subtotal

11 Circle two different numbers which multiply together to make 1 million.

50   200   5000   20 000   100 000   *(1 mark)*

12 Circle all the multiples of 9 in the list of numbers.

19   29   36   51   81   *(1 mark)*

13 Complete the diagram below to make a shape that is symmetrical about the mirror line.

Use a ruler. You may also use a mirror or tracing paper.

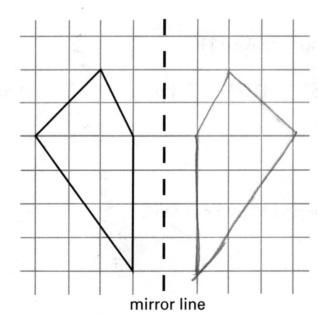

mirror line

(1 mark)

14 This table shows the heights of four children.

Complete the table.

	cm	m
Jake	150	1.5
Sue	139	1.39
Alice	1 15	1.15
Rosie	135	1.35

(2 marks)

15 Calculate 5.7 – 2.15 [ ]

(1 mark)

16 Write in the missing digit to make this correct.

```
    3  2  4
  ×      [  ]
  _____
  1  6  2  0
```

(1 mark)

Turn over

17 Draw two more straight sides to make a rectangle.

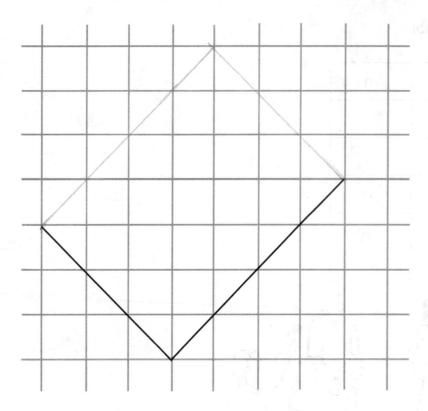

(1 mark)

Q17

18 Two of these numbers divide by 7 with no remainder.

Circle the two numbers.

17   24   28   31   37   49   *(1 mark)*

Q18

19 Calculate 35% of £560   £   *(1 mark)*

Q19

20 Here is a kite drawn on a graph.

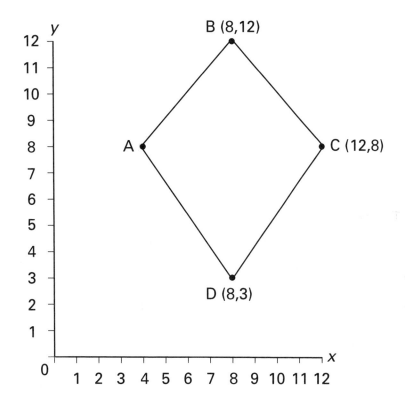

What are the coordinates of point A?

(☐ , ☐)

(1 mark)

21 Calculate 12.15 − 11.84

(1 mark)

Turn over

22 Jane has some rectangular tiles like this.

12 cm

←5 cm→

She then makes this T shape.

(handwritten annotations: 12, 5, 5, 2.5, 2.5, 8, 12, 12, 5)

a) **What is the perimeter of Jane's T shape?** [ ] cm   *(1 mark)*

She then puts two T shapes together.

b) **What is the perimeter of Jane's new shape?** [ ] cm   *(1 mark)*

23 This is an isosceles triangle.

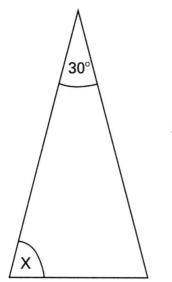

How many degrees is angle x? °

(1 mark)

Q23

24 Draw lines to match the circles which are equal in value.

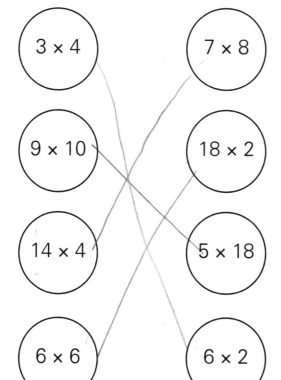

(2 marks)

Q24

subtotal

25 Calculate $1047 - 259$ ☐

(1 mark) ☐
Q25

26 Here are five shapes on a square grid.

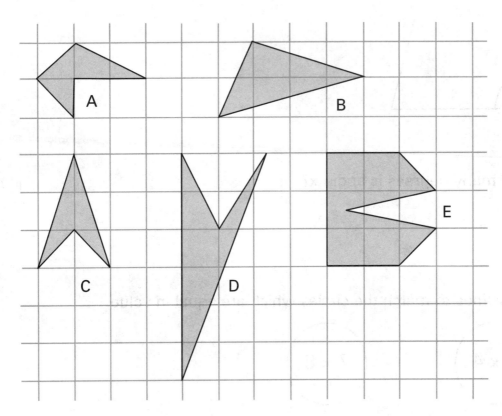

Write the letters of the two shapes which have a line of symmetry.

☐ and ☐

(2 marks) ☐
Q26

This is the morning timetable for three school buses.

	PARK	SHOPS	POST OFFICE	SCHOOL
BUS 1	07:21	07:39	08:25	08:40
BUS 2	07:55	08:15	08:45	08:59
BUS 3	07:35	08:00	08:20	08:30

a) Which bus arrives at the Post office first? (1 mark)

Q27a

b) How long in minutes does it take for Bus 1 to get from the Park to the Post office? (1 mark)

Q27b

Turn over

subtotal

28 Write each of the following numbers in the correct place on the Venn diagram below.

18   36   26

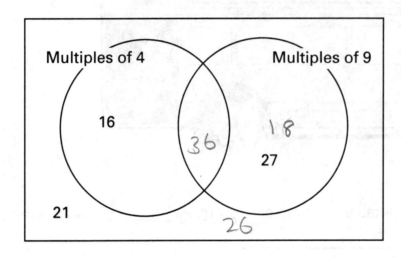

(2 marks)

29 Here is a sorting diagram for numbers.

Write a number greater than 50 but less than 200 in each space.

	odd	not odd
a multiple of 9	81	90
a multiple of 7	63	84

(2 marks)

END OF TEST

Sets
ABC

KEY STAGE 2
Levels 3–5

Instructions,
Answers and
Mark Scheme
Booklet

Maths

Instructions and Answers

Instructions, Answers and Mark Scheme Booklet

This booklet provides advice on how to use the tests, as well as supplies the answers and the mark schemes for each of the test papers.

On page 15 of this booklet, there is a grid to fill in, to record your marks, and a guide showing how your marks relate to levels.

Contents

Instructions on using the Practice Papers

Understanding the SATs

What are the SATs?

SATs are taken by pupils at the end of Year 2 in English and Mathematics. Teacher assessments will form the main part of the child's result. However, National Tests will validate the teacher's own assessment. There are no tests in Science until Year 6.

What are the children tested on?

The children are tested on all of the work they have covered in all year groups so far. Year 6 children are tested on Maths, English and Science. Years 3, 4 and 5 are only tested in Maths and English, and have Science assessments throughout the year.

What SATs will my child take?

The exact format of the tests depends on the year, but this is a typical breakdown:

English **Reading** (45 minutes + 15 mins reading time) **Writing** Long 45 minutes and short 20 minutes **Spelling** 10 mins **Handwriting**

Maths **Mental Maths** (20 minutes) **Written paper** (45 minutes) **Written paper** (45 minutes)

Science Year 6 only Science (paper A) 45 minutes Science (paper B) 45 minutes

* No statutory testing is carried out at KS1.

What do the Maths tests assess in my child?

All children study the National Curriculum from Year 1. At the end of each Key Stage, the tests will assess your child's knowledge, skills and understanding in the programmes of study that they have followed.

In Mathematics, the Programme of Study covers four areas or Attainment Targets:

Mathematics 1:   Using and applying mathematics

Mathematics 2:   Number and algebra

Mathematics 3:   Space, shape and measures

Mathematics 4:   Handling data

Can my child fail a SATs test?

It is important that children understand they are not going to 'pass' or 'fail' the test - it will just show what they have learned and what they can do.

About these Practice Papers

1   These test papers are similar to the one your child will take at the end of Year 6. The papers provide a good idea of strengths and weaknesses of your child's subject knowledge.

2   The answers and mark scheme have been provided to allow you to check how your child has done.

3   When an area of weakness has been identified, it is useful to go over these and similar types of questions with your child. Sometimes your child will be familiar with the subject matter but might not understand what the question is asking. This will become apparent when talking to your child.

Tips for the top

1   Don't make silly mistakes. Make sure you emphasise to your child the importance of reading the question. Easy marks can be picked up by just doing as the question asks.

2   Make your answers clearly legible. If your child has made a mistake, encourage them to put a cross through it and write the correct answer clearly next to it. Try to encourage your child to use an eraser as little as possible.

3   Don't panic! These practice papers, and the end of Key Stage 2 SATs, are meant to provide teachers with a guide to the level a child has aspired to. They are not the be all and end all. Explain to your child that there is no need to worry if they cannot do a question, just go on to the next question and come back to it later if they have time.

Taking the Tests

1   Make sure you provide your child with a quiet environment where they can complete their test undisturbed.

2   Provide your child with the following equipment: pencil, ruler, eraser (rubber), small mirror, tracing paper and an angle measurer (protractor). You will also need a calculator for Test Paper 2.

3   Test Papers 1 and 2 are both 45 minutes long. The mental arithmetic paper will take about 20 minutes.

4   Explain to your child before the test starts to show their working in the boxes that are clearly marked on the test papers. See below:

> Show your working. You may get a mark.

5   Always show working. This may get a mark.

Set A Test Paper 1 Answers

1) a) 1000 *(1 mark)*
    b) 10.4 *(1 mark)*

2) $\frac{3}{8}$ – accept $\frac{6}{16}$ *(1 mark)*
    Note to parent *This question is concerned with* **Fractions**. *It is important that your child recognises that $\frac{3}{8}$ is the same as $\frac{6}{16}$.*

3) a) 3 *(1 mark)*
    b) £4.02 *(1 mark)*
    Note to parent *This question is all about* **Addition** *and doubling. Make sure your child knows that 99p can be rounded up to £1 to make the question easier.*

4) 135   165 *(1 mark)*

5) 11:20 or twenty past eleven *(1 mark)*
    Note to parent *If your child struggles with time, practise this type of question with different increments of 5 minutes.*

6) 28 m   80 km
    Both answers must be correct. *(1 mark)*

7) a) 70 *(1 mark)*
    b) CAT   DOG   (FISH)

    Accept any other way as long as fish is clearly marked. *(1 mark)*
    Note to parent *It is important that your child understands that* **45 + 12 + 9 + 4 = 70**, *i.e. all the numbers inside the* **Dogs** *circle.*

8) a) Accept 103–109 mm *(1 mark)*
    b) Accept 52°–58° *(1 mark)*
    Note to parent *This question concerns measuring accurately. Practise by drawing some lines and angles on some paper.*

9) (0.24) 0.09 0.9 0.51 (0.57) 0.17 *(1 mark)*

10)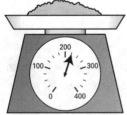

    Note to parent *Practise reading scales by weighing different objects on either kitchen or bathroom scales.*

11) 50 (200) (5000) 20 000   100 000
    OR
    (50) 200   5000 (20 000) 100 000

    (1 mark)

12) 19   29   (36)   51   (81)

    Both answers must be circled. *(1 mark)*

13) *(1 mark)*
    Note to parent *Make sure your child used a mirror when doing this question.*

14)
	cm	m
Jake	150	**1.5**
Sue	139	**1.39**
Alice	**115**	1.15
Rosie	135	1.35

(three correct gets 2 marks, two correct gets 1 mark)
Note to parent *Converting from cm to m is all about moving the decimal point. Explain this to your child and give them plenty of practice.*

15) 3.55 *(1 mark)*

16) 5 *(1 mark)*

17) 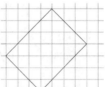 *(1 mark)*

18) 28 and 49. Both must be correct. *(1 mark)*

19) £196 *(1 mark)*
    Note to parent *Give your child plenty of practice at* **Percentages**. *Let them check their answers on a calculator after they have completed the test.*

20) (4, 8) *(1 mark)*

21) 0.31 *(1 mark)*
    Note to parent *This question involves* **Subtraction**. *Because the numbers are close together, the easiest method is to* **count on** *from the* **smallest** *number.*

22) a) 58 cm *(1 mark)*
    b) 106 cm *(1 mark)*

23) 75° *(1 mark)*
    Note to parent *It is important that your child understands 'isosceles' is a triangle with two equal angles and two equal sides. Also a triangle always has 180° in total.*

24)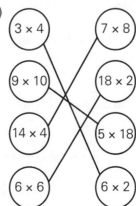

(2 marks for all 4 correct, 1 mark for 2 or 3 correct)

25) 788 *(1 mark)*

26) C and E *(2 marks)*
Note to parent *A mirror is a necessity here. Make sure your child understands the term 'line of symmetry'.*

27) a) Bus 3 *(1 mark)*
    b) 64 mins or 1hr and 4 mins *(1 mark)*

28)

(All three correct gets 2 marks, two correct gets 1 mark)

29) All four correct gets 2 marks, two or three correct gets 1 mark. There are lots of possible answers for this question.

e.g.

81	72
63	56

(up to 2 marks)

Note to parent *Explain to your child that any odd number multiplied by an odd number always equals an odd number.*

Set A Test Paper 2 Answers

1) a) 264 *(1 mark)*
   b) 254 *(1 mark)*
   c) 7 *(1 mark)*
   Note to parent *This question is aimed at testing your child's basic calculator skills. Give your child plenty of practice, especially* **Multiplication** *and* **Division.**

2) *(1 mark)*
   Note to parent *Make sure your child used a mirror when doing this question.*

3) a) $13\frac{1}{2}$ hrs or 13hrs 30mins *(1 mark)*
   b) Friday *(1 mark)*
   c) 100 minutes or 1 hour 40 mins *(1 mark)*

4) a) 30 stamps *(1 mark)*
   b) 13 packs *(1 mark)*
   Note to parent *Problem solving is at the heart of this question. Make sure your child uses a calculator and checks their answer.*

5) a) 692.52 *(1 mark)*
   b) 455.55 *(1 mark)*
   Note to parent *This question is aimed at testing your child's basic calculator skills. Calculations in brackets must* **always** *be completed first.*

6) £2.35
   Correct answer gets 2 marks. 1 mark for working out, e.g. 2 × 6.95 + 3.75 etc. even if incorrect answer given. *(up to 2 marks)*

7) a) 62 *(1 mark)*
   b) Wednesday *(1 mark)*
   Note to parent *Reading graphs can sometimes cause problems. Encourage your child to use a ruler when referencing a point on the graph to either axis. This helps to eliminate errors.*

8) 228 *(1 mark)*
   Note to parent *Encourage your child to use a calculator. It is easy to divide by 7 to get one 7th and then multiply by 4 to get the answer.*

9)

	Has 4 equal angles	Has no right angle	Has an obtuse angle
Has 2 pairs of parallel sides	**C A**	**B**	**B**
Has 1 pair of parallel sides			**D**

(three correct gets 2 marks, two correct gets 1 mark)
Note to parent *Ensure your child knows the terms 'obtuse', 'parallel' and 'right angle'.*

10) Any answer from 48°–52° *(1 mark)*
    Note to parent *This question concerns measuring accurately. Practise by drawing and measuring angles on some paper.*

11) 8   2048 *(2 marks)*

12) a) 4500 m *(1 mark)*
    b) 130 seconds or 2 minutes and 10 seconds *(1 mark)*

13) 108 sq cm
2 marks for correct answer;
1 mark if working out shows an understanding
of perimeter and area.   *(up to 2 marks)*
Note to parent *Ensure your child understands the
terms 'area' and 'perimeter'.*

14) 648   *(1 mark)*
Note to parent *This question is about the
relationship of **Percentages** and **Decimals**. It is
important that your child realises that **45% is the
same as 0.45**. Make sure they use a calculator.*

15) a) 21   *(1 mark)*
b) 7   *(1 mark)*
Note to parent *This question is aimed at testing
your child's basic calculator skills. Calculations in
brackets must **always** be completed first.*

16)   *(2 marks)*

	7	7	8
–		8	7
	6	9	1

Note to parent *It is
important that your child
recognises that they must
work from the right-hand
side when working out the
answer here.*

17) a) £12.40 per adult   *(1 mark)*
b) £296
1 mark awarded if method is correct, e.g.
188.5 ÷ 29 = 6.5 then multiply by 7 to get
the extra cost etc.   *(2 marks)*

18) a) 44 kg   *(1 mark)*
b) 7 kg   *(1 mark)*
Note to parent *Practise reading scales by weighing
different objects on either kitchen or bathroom scales.*

19) 129   97   (420)   270   235   *(1 mark)*

20) 45°   *(1 mark)*
Note to parent *It is important that your child knows
that the total of the angles in a triangle is 180°. Also
that an 'isosceles triangle' is a triangle with two equal
angles and two equal sides.*

21) n = 7   *(1 mark)*

22)

	prime number	square number	negative number
(587 – 459) ÷ 2		✔	
(28.9 – 18.9) – 3	✔		
(2.9 × 3.7) – 12			✔
9 + (8 × 6) + 24		✔	

(up to 2 marks)

2 marks if all four are correct.
1 mark if two or three are correct.
Note to parent *Ensure that your child knows the
terms 'prime number', 'square number' and 'negative
number'. Make sure that they calculate the numbers
in the brackets first.*

Set A Mental Arithmetic Test Paper Answers

1) 2060	6) £4.20	11) 195 mins	16) 71
2) 30	7) 24	12) 180	17) 44
3) 820	8) 2	13) 225	18) £15
4) 37	9) $\frac{9}{10}$	14) 3.3	19) 5600
5) 52	10) 56 cm	15) 120	20) 85°

Set B Test Paper 1 Answers

1) a) 17   *(1 mark)*
b) 65   *(1 mark)*

2) 8:05 or five past eight   *(1 mark)*
Note to parent *If your child struggles with time,
practise this type of question with different
increments of 5 minutes.*

3) (11, 5)   *(1 mark)*
Note to parent *Ensure your child understands the
term 'parallelogram', i.e. four–sided shape with
opposite sides being parallel to each other.*

4) 75   150
Both answers must be correct.   *(1 mark)*

5) a) Accept 15–20 girls   *(1 mark)*

b) Male – accept any explanation along the
lines of more shaded area on the
diagram for the males or approximate
numbers larger.   *(1 mark)*

6) 12°C   *(1 mark)*

7) 53
2 marks for the correct answer; 1 mark for
any method that shows a logical way of
getting to the correct answer.   *(up to 2 marks)*
Note to parent *This is a complicated division. The
easiest solution would be to work with lots of 140s
(10 × 14) and add them together until the correct
answer is near. Lots of practice of these types of
problems is needed. Children can then check their
answers with a calculator.*

8) Any of these: 947, 749, 927, 729   *(1 mark)*

9)   *(1 mark)*

Note to parent *Make sure your child used a mirror when doing this question.*

10) 29**7** + 4**8**7 = 784   *(1 mark)*

11) a) x = 35°   *(1 mark)*
     b) y = 145°   *(1 mark)*
     Note to parent *With this question it is important that your child knows that the angle about a straight horizontal line from any point is 180°. (35° + 145° = 180°).*

12) a) £2 or 200p   *(1 mark)*
     b) 480 g or 0.48 kg
         2 marks awarded for the correct answer;
         1 mark for a valid method, e.g. £1.60 is
         4 bags, 4 × 120 g etc.   *(2 marks)*

13)

	grams	kilos
Amy	37 000	37
Alex	**31 500**	31.5
Ben	40 500	**40.5**
Charlie	**37 020**	37.02

All three correct for 2 marks.
Two correct for 1 mark.

(up to 2 marks)
Note to parent *Converting from grams to kilos is all about moving the decimal point. Explain this to your child and give them plenty of practice.*

14) 54 cm   *(1 mark)*
     Note to parent *Make sure your child knows that an equilateral triangle has three equal sides and angles.*

15)
```
  47    (48)    49
  50     51     52
  53    (54)    55
  56     57     58
  59    (60)    61
  62     63     64
```
(1 mark)

16) Accept 7.9 cm – 8.1 cm   *(1 mark)*

17) 1.06   *(1 mark)*
     Note to parent *This question involves **Subtraction**. Because the numbers are close together the easiest method is to **count on** from the **smallest** number.*

18) 411   *(1 mark)*

19)   *(1 mark)*

20) 896   *(1 mark)*

21) 17 (21)(35) 47 36   *(1 mark)*

Both answers need to be correct.

22)

All three correct gets 2 marks. Two correct gets 1 mark.
(up to 2 marks)

23) All four correct gets 2 marks. Two or three correct gets 1 mark. There are lots of possible answers to this question.

e.g.

24	36
40	64

(up to 2 marks)
Note to parent *Ensure your child knows what a square number is.*

24) $\dfrac{2}{4}$ $\dfrac{1}{2}$ $\dfrac{4}{8}$ $\dfrac{16}{32}$

Also accept any whole number variations. All four must be correct to get 2 marks. Two or three correct gets 1 mark.   *(up to 2 marks)*

25) 294
     Correct answer gets 2 marks. If a valid method to work out the answer is shown, 1 mark is awarded.   *(up to 2 marks)*
     Note to parent *Encourage your child to break down the numbers into more manageable amounts, i.e. 21 × 14 = (10 × 14) + (10 × 14) + (1 × 14)*

26) a)   *(1 mark)*

     b) 525 grams   *(1 mark)*

27) Shapes C and D:
     1 mark for each correct answer. *(up to 2 marks)*

Set B Test Paper 2 Answers

1) (850) 720 951 970 90   *(1 mark)*

2) 148°–150°   *(1 mark)*
   Note to parent *This question concerns measuring accurately. Practise by drawing and measuring angles on some paper.*

3) a)   *(1 mark)*

   b)   *(1 mark)*

   c)   *(1 mark)*

4) a) 301   *(1 mark)*
   b) 428   *(1 mark)*
   c) 9   *(1 mark)*
   Note to parent *This question is aimed at testing your child's basic calculator skills. Give your child plenty of practice, especially **Multiplication** and **Division**.*

5) All four correct gets 2 marks. Two or three correct gets 1 mark. There are lots of possible answers for this question.

   e.g.
630	300
502	309

   (up to 2 marks)

6) £2.60
   Correct answer gets 2 marks. Any valid working out gets 1 mark, e.g. 45 × 2 + 150 then 500 – 240 or something similar.
   (up to 2 marks)

7) 1344   *(1 mark)*
   Note to parent *This question is about the relationship of **Percentages** and **Decimals**. It is important that your child realises that **80% is the same as 0.80**. Make sure they use a calculator.*

8) a) 120 km   *(1 mark)*
   b) 65 km accept 62 km – 66 km   *(1 mark)*
   Note to parent *Reading graphs can sometimes cause problems. Encourage your child to use a ruler when referencing a point on the graph to either axis. This helps to eliminate errors.*

9) a) 25.5   *(1 mark)*
   b) 180.95   *(1 mark)*
   Note to parent *This question is aimed at testing your child's basic calculator skills. Calculations in brackets must **always** be completed first.*

10) Accept any square with an area of 9 squares.
    (1 mark)
    Note to parent *A common mistake is for a child to always picture a square like this, ☐ , whereas in this case it is easier to draw a diamond shape, ◇ , like this.*

11)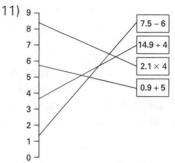

    1 mark awarded for each correct answer. *(3 marks)*

12) 168   *(1 mark)*
    Note to parent *Encourage your child to use a calculator. It is easy to divide by 9 to get one-ninth and then multiply by 2 to get the answer.*

13) a) 6 boxes   *(1 mark)*
    b) 12 eggs   *(1 mark)*

14)   *(1 mark)*
    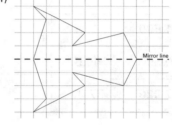

    Note to parent
    Make sure your child used a mirror when doing this question.

15) 24   921   *(2 marks)*

16) a) red   *(1 mark)*
    b) 59   *(1 mark)*

17) a) 38   *(1 mark)*
    b) 100   *(1 mark)*
    Note to parent *This problem requires your child to use basic calculator skills. Practice of similar problems is recommended if they find this type of problem difficult.*

18) a) 33°C   *(1 mark)*
    b) 37°C   *(1 mark)*
    Note to parent *In this problem your child will need an understanding of negative numbers and such numbers lie below the zero line. E.g. the difference between –10 and 15 is, counting on from –10, 10 to zero and 15 from zero to 15 (10 + 15 = 25).*

19) a) £0.66 or 66p   *(1 mark)*
    b) £5.28
    Correct answer gets 2 marks. 1 mark awarded for a valid method, e.g.
    £7.92 ÷ 3 = $\frac{1}{3}$, John pays the rest etc.
    (2 marks)

20) 828 feet
Correct answer gets 2 marks.
1 mark awarded for a valid method, e.g. convert yards into feet and then work out the perimeter or vice versa. *(up to 2 marks)*

21) r = 80
t = 20 *(2 marks)*

Set B Mental Arithmetic Test Paper Answers

1) 6
2) 45
3) 1930
4) 35
5) 700

6) $4\frac{3}{4}$
7) 14.6
8) 17
9) 40
10) five past six or 6:05

11) 9 cm
12) 0.38
13) 8
14) 108
15) 3 kg

16) 4
17) 4.1
18) £2.80
19) 75°
20) 162

Set C Test Paper 1 Answers

1) 50 *(1 mark)*

2) 365 *(1 mark)*

3) $\dfrac{2}{6}$ $\dfrac{1}{3}$ $\dfrac{9}{27}$ $\dfrac{5}{15}$

or $\dfrac{4}{6}$ $\dfrac{2}{3}$ $\dfrac{18}{27}$ $\dfrac{10}{15}$ *(up to 2 marks)*

Or any whole number derivatives.
Four must be correct to get 2 marks.
Two or three correct gets 1 mark.

4) £5.98 *(1 mark)*

5) 0.4 (0.04) 0.13 0.15 (0.25) 0.09 *(1 mark)*

Note to parent *Most children will get this answer through trial and error. The last digit must be 9, so 0.13 and 0.09 can be discounted straight away. 0.4 is too big, so that leaves only three possible numbers.*

6) 894 *(1 mark)*

7) a) 96 cm *(1 mark)*
b) 64 cm *(1 mark)*
Note to parent *Ensure your child knows the meaning of 'perimeter'.*

8) *(1 mark)*

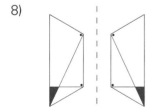
mirror | line

Note to parent *Make sure your child used a mirror when doing this question.*

9) 33**9** + 5**8**6 = 925 *(1 mark)*

10) 85 kilos
Accept kg or kilograms. Only 1 mark awarded if the units are incorrect.
(up to 2 marks)
Note to parent *Practise reading scales by weighing different objects on either kitchen or bathroom scales.*

11) (88) 97 74 (92) (86) (91) *(1 mark)*

All four must be correct to get the mark.
Note to parent *It is important that your child realises they can round down as well as up. Ensure they check each number in turn.*

12) a) Accept 28 mm – 30 mm *(1 mark)*
b) Accept 35° – 39° *(1 mark)*
Note to parent *This question concerns measuring accurately. Practise by drawing some lines and angles on some paper.*

13) 106 *(1 mark)*

14) 54 cm
2 marks if the correct answer is given; 1 mark for a valid method, e.g. 72 ÷ 4 = then × by 3.
(up to 2 marks)

15) **1** 8 **4** *(1 mark)*
   + 5 3 7
   ‾‾‾‾‾‾‾
     7 2 1

16) 23 (30) 46 (48) (60) *(1 mark)*

Note to parent *A thorough knowledge of times tables is needed for this type of question. Practise two different tables every week to improve your child's response times.*

17)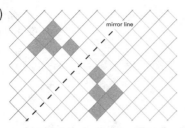
(1 mark)

18) 103.87 *(1 mark)*

19) a) £3.50. Do not accept £350 or £350p *(1 mark)*
    b) £58 *(1 mark)*

20) 10 and 200 000 *(1 mark)*

21) 25% do not accept $\frac{1}{4}$. *(1 mark)*
    Note to parent *It is important that your child knows that $\frac{1}{4}$ and $\frac{4}{16}$ are the same, and also that they are equivalent to 25%. Give your child some practice converting basic fractions to %.*

22)

	mm	cm
pencil 1	230	23
pencil 2	195	**19.5**
pencil 3	**180**	18
pencil 4	**174**	17.4

Three correct gets 2 marks, two correct gets 1 mark. *(2 marks)*
Note to parent *Converting from mm to cm is all about moving the decimal point. Explain this to your child and give them plenty of practice.*

23) 0.29 *(1 mark)*
    Note to parent *This question involves **Subtraction**. Because the numbers are close together the easiest method is to **count on** from the **smallest** number.*

24)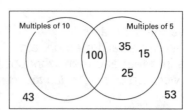
All three correct gets 2 marks. Two correct gets 1 mark. *(up to 2 marks)*

25) £90 *(1 mark)*
    Note to parent *The easiest way to do this question is to find the value of 10% and then halve it.*

26) All four correct gets 2 marks. Two or three correct gets 1 mark. There are lots of possible answers for this question.
    e.g.

40	45
110	33

(up to 2 marks)

27) 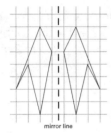 *(1 mark)*

28) a) Josh £2.50
       Ben £1.50 *(1 mark)*
    b) Ben £2.50 *(1 mark)*

29) £254
    Correct answer gets 2 marks. 1 mark given for a valid method, e.g. 5.5 × 40 + 8.5 × 4 etc.
    (up to 2 marks)

Set C Test Paper 2 Answers

1) *(1 mark)*

mirror line

2) (85) 150 215 515 511 *(1 mark)*

3) 15 packs (6 × 100 + 9 × 40)
   2 marks for the correct answer; 1 mark for a valid method only – answer incorrect.
   (up to 2 marks)

4) a) 27 mm *(1 mark)*
   b) 26 mm *(1 mark)*

5) a) 7 *(1 mark)*
   b) 344.34 *(1 mark)*
   Note to parent *This question is aimed at testing your child's basic calculator skills. Calculations in brackets must **always** be completed first.*

6) £1.10
   2 marks if the correct answer is given; 1 mark for a valid method,
   e.g. 3 × 75 + 2 × 40 + 3 × 35 = then take away 300. *(up to 2 marks)*

7) 13 [25] [37] [49] *(up to 2 marks)*

8) a) 25 minutes past 12 or 12:25 *(1 mark)*
   b) 19:13 or 13 minutes past seven *(1 mark)*
   Note to parent *If your child struggles with time, practise this type of question with different increments of 5 minutes.*

9) 117 *(1 mark)*
   Note to parent *This question is about the relationship of **Percentages** and **Decimals**. It is important that your child realises that 30% **is the same as 0.30**. Make sure they use a calculator.*

10) Line CD is parallel to line EF   ✘
    Line BC is parallel to line AF   ✔
    Angle F is a right angle   ✘
    Angle E is obtuse   ✔

(up to 2 marks)

2 marks if all four are correct; 1 mark if two or three are correct.

Note to parent *Ensure your child knows the terms 'obtuse', 'parallel' and 'right angle'.*

11) a) *(1 mark)*

  b) 165 ml   *(1 mark)*

    Note to parent *Make sure your child practises reading scales and division if they struggled with this one. You can get your child to practise reading scales by using a measuring jug and putting different amounts of coloured water in it.*

12) Accept 113° – 117°   *(1 mark)*
    Note to parent *This question concerns measuring accurately. Practise by drawing and measuring angles on some paper.*

13) All four correct gets 2 marks. Two or three correct gets 1 mark. There are lots of possible answers for this question.

    e.g.

70	700
21	217

(up to 2 marks)

14) 54 cm
    2 marks if the correct answer is given; 1 mark for a valid method, e.g. length of 1 side $27 \div 3 = 9$, 1 side of large triangle is 2×9, perimeter is $3 \times (2 \times 9)$ etc.   *(up to 2 marks)*

15) a) 442   *(1 mark)*
    b) 4   *(1 mark)*
    Note to parent *This question is aimed at testing your child's basic calculator skills.*

16) a) $2\frac{1}{2}$ minutes or 2 mins 30 secs   *(1 mark)*
    b) 60°C   *(1 mark)*
    Note to parent *Reading graphs can sometimes cause problems. Encourage your child to use a ruler when referencing a point on the graph to either axis. This helps to eliminate errors.*

17) 360   *(1 mark)*

18) 16   *(1 mark)*

19)   *1 mark for each correct answer.*

(up to 2 marks)

    scalene   (scalene)
    equilateral   equilateral
    (isosceles)   isosceles

Note to parent *Ensure your child understands the terms 'scalene', 'equilateral' and 'isosceles'.*

20) a) £41.82
    2 marks if the correct answer is given; 1 mark for a valid method,
    e.g. $6 \times 2.99 + 12 \times 1.99 =$ answer
(up to 2 marks)
    b) 13 people   *(1 mark)*

21) a)

(1 mark)
    Accept any triangle that is clearly scalene.
    b)   *(1 mark)*

    Accept any triangle that is clearly isosceles.

22) x = 30 y = 40 z = 90
    1 mark for each correct answer. *(up to 3 marks)*

Set C Mental Arithmetic Test Paper Answers

1) $\frac{1}{3}$
2) 14 000 ml
3) 54
4) 16:20
5) 7
6) 550
7) 936
8) 740
9) 600
10) 645 mins
11) 32 m
12) 21
13) 3
14) 30
15) 75 mins or 1 hour and a quarter
16) 48
17) 6.3
18) £38
19) £1.44
20) 6300

Set A – Mental Arithmetic Test

Read out the instructions then each set of questions. The answer sheet is on page 16 of Set A Test Paper 2. The answers are on page 6 of this booklet.

For this group of questions you have 5 seconds to write down each answer.

1   Write in figures the number two thousand and sixty.

2   How many two pence pieces in sixty pence?

3   Add thirty to seven hundred and ninety.

4   Halve seventy-four.

5   Divide five hundred and twenty by ten.

For the next group of questions you get 10 seconds to write down each answer.

6   Jack buys a drink for eighty pence, and pays with a five pound note. How much change does he get?

7   Jane halves a number. She then takes three away to get nine. What number did she start with?

8   Imagine a cylinder. How many edges does it have?

9   Write down the fractional equivalent of zero point nine.

10   Each side of an octagon is seven centimetres. What is the perimeter?

11   How many minutes in three and a quarter hours?

12   What is three-quarters of two hundred and forty?

13   What is nine multiplied by twenty-five?

14   Subtract one point seven from five.

15   Add together thirty, forty and fifty.

For the next group of questions you get 15 seconds to write down each answer.

16   Add together fifteen, thirty-four and twenty-two.

17   What number is halfway between twenty-seven and sixty-one?

18   A sale has thirty per cent off. Jack spends thirty-five pounds. How much money did he save?

19   Multiply seventy by eighty.

20   There are three angles about a point. Two of the angles are eighty-five degrees and one hundred and ninety degrees. What is the third angle?

Now put down your pen or pencil. The test is finished.

Set B - Mental Arithmetic Test

Read out the instructions then each set of questions. The answer sheet is on page 15 of Set B Test Paper 2. The answers are on page 9 of this booklet.

For this group of questions you get 5 seconds to write down each answer.

1   How many sides has a hexagon?

2   How many minutes in three-quarters of an hour?

3   Subtract seventy from two thousand.

4   Halve seventy.

5   Write six hundred and fifty-two to the nearest hundred.

For the next group of questions you get 10 seconds to write down each answer.

6   Add one and a quarter to three and a half.

7   Write down twice seven point three.

8   When z has the value of six, calculate four z minus seven.

9   Eight times a number is three hundred and twenty. What is the number?

10   My watch shows quarter past five. What time is it in fifty minutes?

11   The perimeter of a regular octagon is seventy-two centimetres. What is the length of each side?

12   Write down the decimal equivalent of thirty-eight per cent.

13   Imagine a cube. How many vertices does it have?

14   Write down the multiple of nine between one hundred and one hundred and ten.

15   What is two thousand seven hundred and eighty grams to the nearest kilogram?

For the next group of questions you get 15 seconds to write down each answer.

16   What is the remainder when sixty-seven is divided by seven?

17   How much smaller is eight point three than twelve point four?

18   Four packets of crisps cost one pound sixty. What will seven packets cost?

19   There are three angles on a straight line. Two of the angles are twenty degrees and eighty-five degrees. What is the third angle?

20   What is eighteen multiplied by nine?

Now put down your pen or pencil. The test is finished.

Set C – Mental Arithmetic Test

Read out the instructions then each set of questions. The answer sheet is on page 16 of Set C Test Paper 2. The answers are on page 11 of this booklet.

For this group of questions you get 5 seconds to write down each answer.

1   What is thirty out of ninety as a fraction?

2   How many millilitres are there in fourteen litres?

3   Multiply six by nine.

4   Write twenty past four pm in the twenty-four hour clock.

5   Divide fifty-six by eight.

For the next group of questions you get 10 seconds to write down each answer.

6   What is the sum of eighty and four hundred and seventy?

7   Take sixty-four from one thousand.

8   Write down double three hundred and seventy.

9   What is three-quarters of eight hundred?

10   How many minutes in ten and three quarter hours?

11   The perimeter of a square field is one hundred and twenty-eight metres. How long is each side?

12   What is seven per cent of three hundred?

13   Imagine an equilateral triangle. How many lines of symmetry does it have?

14   How many thirties are there in nine hundred?

15   The train is due to leave at twenty past three. It leaves at four thirty five. How late is the train?

For the next group of questions you get 15 seconds to write down each answer.

16   What number is forty-seven less than ninety-five?

17   Calculate eleven minus four point seven.

18   Tickets to the football match are: adults fourteen pounds and children eight pounds. How much would it cost for one adult and three children?

19   Six eggs cost one pound eight pence. How much do eight eggs cost?

20   Multiply ninety by seventy.

Now put down your pen or pencil. The test is finished.

Marking the Tests and Assessing Levels

1   Marking the practice papers is quite simple. Just use the answers provided in this booklet for each test.

2   Make sure your child has completed all the relevant tests, e.g. Set A Test Paper 1, Set A Test Paper 2 and Set A Mental Arithmetic Test.

3   Add up the marks on each paper. Test Paper 1 is marked out of 40, Test Paper 2 is marked out of 40 and Mental Arithmetic is marked out of 20. This gives a maximum total of 100 marks.

4   Write the marks in the corresponding table below.

	Test Paper 1	Test Paper 2	Mental	Total
Set A				
Set B				
Set C				

Once you have your total mark out of 100 look at the table below to find out what level that is.

Level 2	Level 3	Level 4	Level 5
15–20	21–50	51–80	81–100

Shared marking and target setting
Engaging your child in the marking process with you will help them to develop a greater understanding of the Maths Tests and, more importantly, provide them with some ownership of their learning.

They will be able to see more clearly how and why certain areas have been identified for them to target for improvement.

Please note: these tests are only a guide to the level your child can achieve and cannot guarantee the same level is achieved during their KS2 SATs.

How well has my child done in these tests?

The results show whether or not your child has reached the expected National Curriculum level for their age.

	Aged 7	Aged 11	Aged 14
Level 1	Below average		
Level 2 Level 2a Level 2b Level 2c	At level expected	Below average	
Level 3	Excellent	Below average	Below average
Level 4	Exceptional	At level expected	Below average
Level 5		Excellent	At level expected
Level 6		Exceptional	At level expected
Level 7			Excellent
Level 8			Exceptional

What do the levels mean?

When your child's Maths papers are marked, the correct marks are collated to give your child an overall score. This score is then matched to a National Curriculum level.

It is expected that the majority of 11 year old children will achieve Level 4 by the end of Year 6. However, for some children achieving Level 3 is a real success for that particular individual. A child achieving Level 5 is working at a high level, and only one percent achieve Level 6. A child who passes GCSE at grade C has achieved level 7.

Set C

KEY STAGE 2
Levels 3–5

Test Paper 1

Maths

Test Paper 1 (calculator **not** allowed)

Test Paper 1 (calculator **not** allowed)

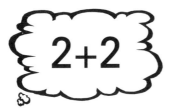

Instructions:

- find a quiet place where you can sit down and complete the test paper undisturbed
- make sure you have all the necessary equipment to complete the test paper
- read the questions carefully
- answer all the questions in this booklet
- go through and check your answers when you have finished the test paper

Time:

This test paper is **45 minutes** long.

Note to Parents:

Check how your child has done against the mark scheme in the Instructions, Answers and Mark Scheme Booklet.

Page	3	5	7	9	11	13	14	Max. Mark	**Actual Mark**
Score	....	....	....	....	....	....	....	40	....

First name ....

Last name ....

1 Write the missing number in the box.

$7 \times \boxed{} = 350$

(1 mark)

Q1

2 Calculate $532 - 167$ $\boxed{}$

(1 mark)

Q2

3 Complete these fractions so that they are equivalent.

$$\overline{6} \qquad\qquad \overline{3} \qquad\qquad \overline{27} \qquad\qquad \overline{15}$$

(2 marks)

Q3

4 DVDs are on offer at the supermarket. The sign says:

1 DVD is £17.99 or buy 2 DVDs for £30

How much money will Sarah save if she buys
two DVDs together instead of buying them separately? £ $\boxed{}$ *(1 mark)*

Q4

5 Circle two numbers which add to make 0.29.

0.4   0.04   0.13   0.15   0.25   0.09   *(1 mark)*   Q5

6 Calculate 1245 – 351 ☐   *(1 mark)*   Q6

7 John has some bricks. Each brick is 10 cm long, 4 cm high and 4 cm deep.

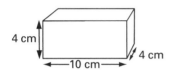

John then builds a square wall using eight bricks like this:

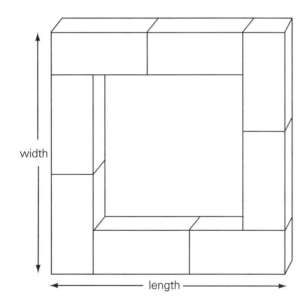

width

length

a) What is the perimeter of the wall?   ☐ cm   *(1 mark)*   Q7a

b) Calculate the inside perimeter of the wall.   ☐ cm   *(1 mark)*   Q7b

8   Here is a trapezium with a design on it.

The trapezium is reflected in the mirror line.

Complete the reflected design.

You may use a mirror or tracing paper.

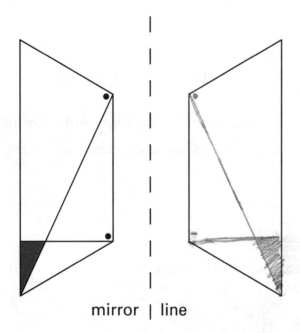

mirror | line

(1 mark)

Q8

9   **Write in the missing digits.**

| 3 | 3 | | + | 5 | | 6 | = | 9 | 2 | 5 |

(1 mark)

Q9

10 Mr Green has three tubs of water.

He weighs them on the garden scales.

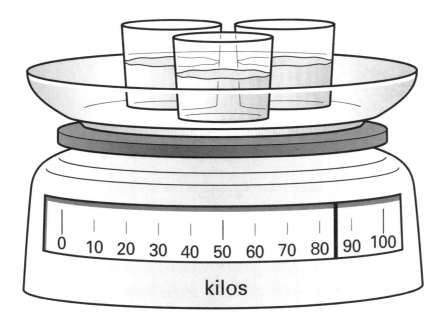

What is the reading on the scale? (2 marks)

11 Which of these numbers give 90 when rounded to the nearest 10?

Circle all the correct numbers.

88   97   74   92   86   91   (1 mark)

Turn over

12 Measure accurately the shortest side of this shape.

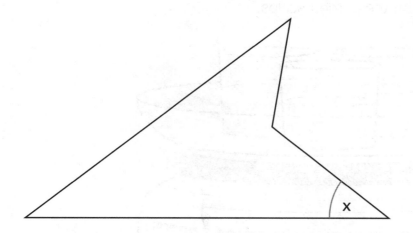

a) Give your answer in millimetres. [   ] mm   *(1 mark)*

b) Measure angle x using a protractor. [   ]°   *(1 mark)*

13 Calculate $954 \div 9$ [   ]   *(1 mark)*

14 Here is an equilateral triangle inside a square.

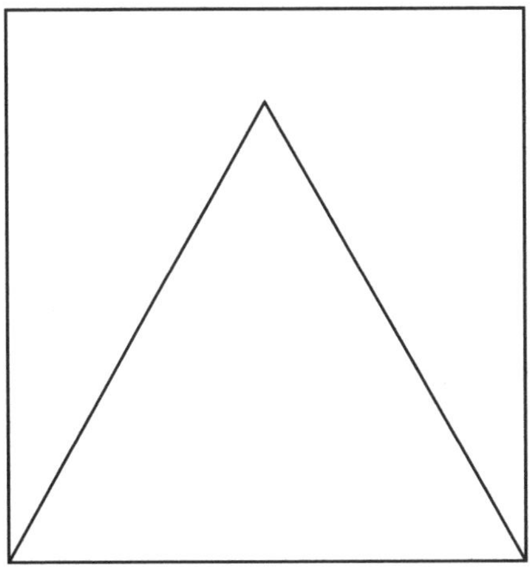

Not actual size.

The perimeter of the square is 72 centimetres.

What is the perimeter of the triangle? ☐ cm

Show your working. You may get a mark.

(2 marks) ☐ Q14

15 **Write in the missing digits to make this correct.**

☐	8	☐
+ 5	3	7
7	2	1

(1 mark) ☐ Q15

Turn over

subtotal

16 Circle all the multiples of 6 in the list of numbers.

23   30   46   48   60

(1 mark)

17 Draw the reflection of the shaded shape in the mirror line.

You may use a mirror or tracing paper.

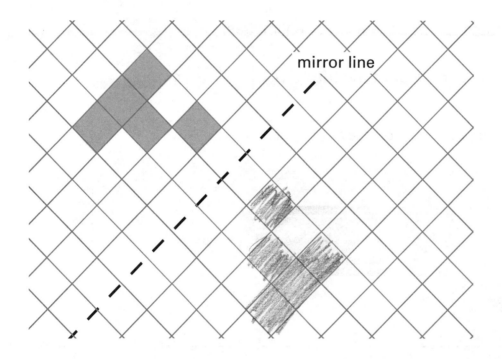

mirror line

(1 mark)

18 Calculate 64.09 + 39.78

(1 mark)

19 This table shows the increase in train fares.

Train fares	
Old fare	New fare
£25.00	£27.50
£28.75	£33.00
£40.00	£44.75
£43.50	£50.00
£47.75	£51.25
£49.00	£58.00
£51.00	£61.50

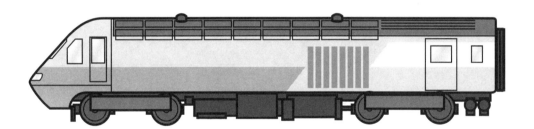

a) Jack's new fare is £51.25.
How much has his fare increased?   £ [　　]   *(1 mark)*

b) Jane's new fare is £9 more than her old fare.
What is her new fare?   £ [　　]   *(1 mark)*

Turn over

subtotal

20 Circle two different numbers which multiply together to make 2 million.

10   500   2000   40 000   200 000   *(1 mark)*

21 Here is a square divided into identical smaller squares.

What percentage of the square is shaded? ☐ %   *(1 mark)*

22 This table shows the lengths of four pencils.

Complete the table.

	mm	cm
pencil 1	230	23
pencil 2	195	
pencil 3		18
pencil 4		17.4

(2 marks)

23 Calculate 9.23 – 8.94

(1 mark)

24 Write each of the following numbers in the correct place on the Venn diagram below.

15   35   53

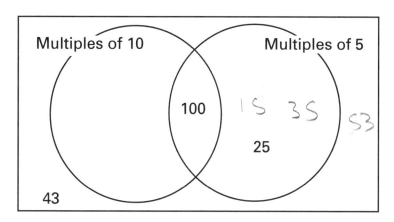

(2 marks)

Turn over

25 Calculate 5% of £1800   £[   ]   *(1 mark)*

Q25

26 Here is a sorting diagram for numbers.

Write a number less than 200 in each space

	even	odd
divides by 5 with no remainder		
divides by 11 with no remainder		

(2 marks)

Q26

27 Jack and Mary are going to the cinema to watch a film. The film starts at **twenty minutes to eight**.

Complete the clock below to show the time that the film starts.

(1 mark)

Q27

28 Three children have £2 each.

Ellie   Josh   Ben

Ben gives Josh $\frac{1}{4}$ of his money.

a) How much money do Josh and Ben have now?

Josh £ ☐

Ben £ ☐

(1 mark)

Q28a

b) Ellie spends 50% of her money and gives the remainder to Ben.

How much money does Ben have now?

Ben £ ☐

(1 mark)

Q28b

Turn over

subtotal

29 The children in Year 5 go on a class trip to a theme park.

There are 40 children in Year 5 and four teachers go on the trip as well.

What is the total cost for the group to enter the theme park? £

Show your working. You may get a mark.

(2 marks)

Q29

subtotal

END OF TEST

Set **B**

KEY STAGE 2
Levels 3–5

Test Paper 2

Maths

Test Paper 2 (calculator allowed)
& Mental Arithmetic Test

Test Paper 2 (calculator allowed)
& Mental Arithmetic Test

Instructions:

- find a quiet place where you can sit down and complete the test paper undisturbed
- make sure you have all the necessary equipment to complete the test paper
- read the questions carefully
- answer all the questions in this booklet
- go through and check your answers when you have finished the test paper

Time:

This test paper is **45 minutes** long.

Note to Parents:

Check how your child has done against the mark scheme in the Instructions, Answers and Mark Scheme Booklet.

Page	3	5	7	9	11	13	14	Max. Mark	**Actual Mark**
Score	....	....	....	....	....	....	....	40	....

Mental Arithmetic Test

Max. Mark	**Actual Mark**
20	....

First name ....

Last name ....

1 Circle the number that is closest to 900.

850   720   951   970   90   *(1 mark)*

2

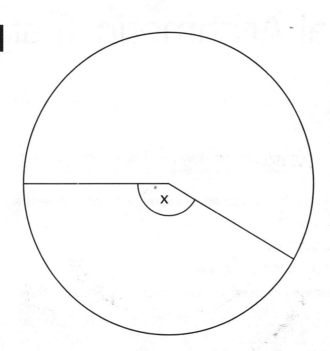

Measure the angle x accurately.

Use an angle measurer (a protractor).   *(1 mark)*

3 Show the correct time on the clocks below.

An example has been done for you.

half past three

a) quarter to six

(1 mark) ☐
Q3a

b) 11:25

(1 mark) ☐
Q3b

c) 23:45

(1 mark) ☐
Q3c

Turn over

subtotal

4 Write the missing numbers in the boxes.

a) $\boxed{} \div 7 = 43$ *(1 mark)*

b) $539 - \boxed{} = 111$ *(1 mark)*

c) $\boxed{} \times 31 = 279$ *(1 mark)*

5 Here is a diagram for sorting numbers.

Write one number in each section of the diagram.

	more than 500	less than 500
multiple of 30		
not a multiple of 30		

(2 marks)

6 These are the prices of some games at the school summer fair.

welly throwing	**45p**
lucky dip	**30p**
face painting	**£1.50**
dance mats	**£1.00**

Sally has **£5**. She has her **face painted** and then has **two**
tries at **welly throwing**. How much money does she have left?   £ [   ]

Show your working. You may get a mark.

(2 marks)

Q6

7 Calculate **80% of 1680** [   ]   *(1 mark)*

Q7

8   Joe took part in a sponsored cycle ride.

This graph shows how far he rode and how long it took him.

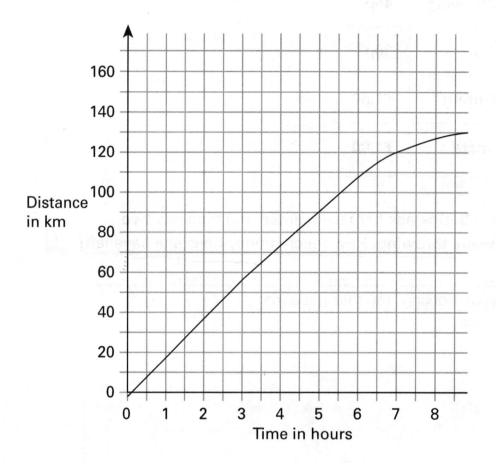

a) Look at the graph. How far
   had Joe ridden after seven hours?   ☐ km   *(1 mark)*   ☐

Q8a

b) Joe started riding at 8:30 in the morning.
   How far had he gone at 12:00pm?   ☐ km   *(1 mark)*   ☐

Q8b

9   Write the missing numbers in the boxes.

a) 502.35 ÷ ☐ = 19.7   *(1 mark)*   ☐

Q9a

b) (49.7 − 23.85) × 7 = ☐   *(1 mark)*   ☐

Q9b

10 On the grid below, draw a square with the same area as the shaded shape.

Use a ruler.

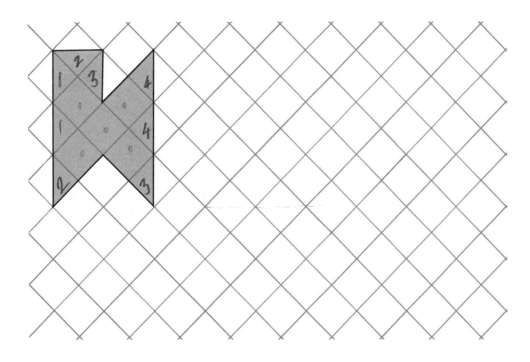

(1 mark)

11 Draw a line from each card to the correct part of the number line.

The first one has been done for you.

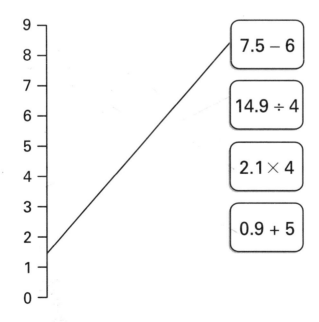

7.5 − 6

14.9 ÷ 4

2.1 × 4

0.9 + 5

(3 marks)

Turn over

12 Calculate $\frac{2}{9}$ of 756 ⬜

13 At the supermarket eggs are for sale in boxes of six.

John needs 36 eggs for the egg and spoon race at school.

a) **How many boxes of eggs does John need?** ⬜ boxes   *(1 mark)*

John breaks $\frac{1}{3}$ of the eggs when he drops the boxes.

b) **How many eggs does John break?** ⬜ eggs   *(1 mark)*

14 Complete the diagram below to make a shape that is **symmetrical** about the **mirror line**.

You may use a mirror or tracing paper.

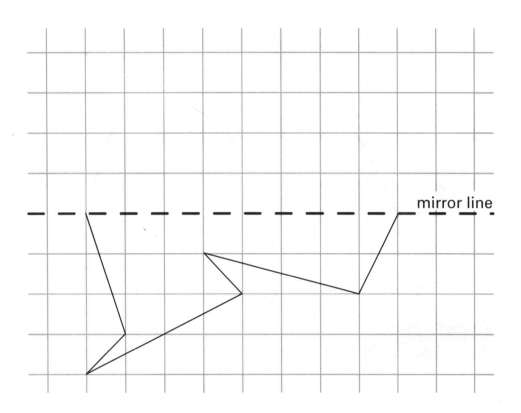

mirror line

(1 mark)

15 Harry makes a sequence of numbers.

His rule is:

Add seven to the previous number, then multiply by 3.

Write in the missing numbers of his sequence.

1 ☐ 93 300 ☐

(2 marks)

Turn over

subtotal

16 Some children at school did a survey on the colour of their parents' cars.

The results of the survey are shown in the table below.

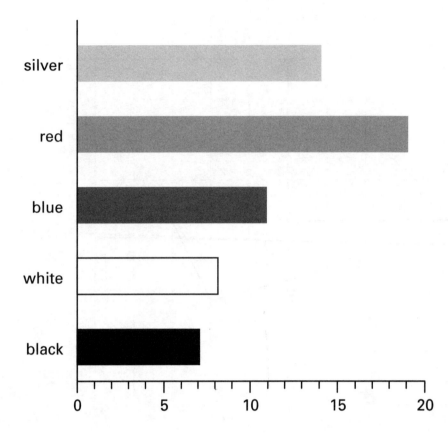

a) Which car colour has eight **more than** blue? _(1 mark)_ Q16a

b) What is the **total** number of cars in the survey? _(1 mark)_ Q16b

17 Write the missing numbers in the boxes.

a) $(5 \times 9) + 97 - 104 =$ _(1 mark)_ Q17a

b) $- 41 + 120 = 179$ _(1 mark)_ Q17b

18 Write the temperature shown on the thermometer.

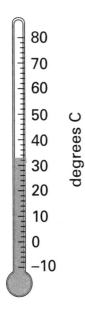

a) [   ] °C

Here is another thermometer.

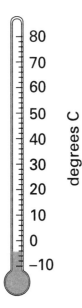

b) What is the difference between
the two temperature readings? [   ] °C

Turn over

19

A box of twelve golf balls costs **£7.92**.

a) **How much does each ball cost?**

(1 mark)

Q19a

John wants eight golf balls and Tom wants four golf balls.

John and Tom both pay some money towards the golf balls.
Tom pays a third of the cost.

b) **How much money does John pay?** £

Show your working. You may get a mark.

(2 marks)

Q19b

20 Here is a football pitch.

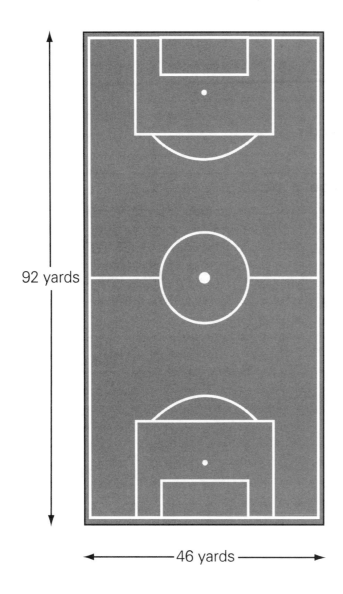

92 yards

← 46 yards →

One yard is **equivalent** to three feet.

What is the perimeter of the pitch? Give your answer in feet. [ ] feet

Show your working. You may get a mark.

(2 marks)

21 t and r each stand for a whole number.

$r - t = 60$

r is **four times** bigger than t.

Calculate the numbers for t and r.

Show your working. You may get a mark.

r = [   ]   t = [   ]

(2 marks)

END OF TEST

subtotal

Set B – Mental Arithmetic Test

The questions for this test are on page 13 of the Instructions, Answers and Mark Scheme Booklet.

Time: 5 seconds

1. [ ] HOW MANY SIDES HAS A HEXAGON [ ]

2. [ ] Hom MANY MINNTES in $\frac{3}{4}$ of an hour [ ]

3. [ ] Subtract 705 from 2000 [ ]

4. [ ] HALVE 70 [ ]

5. [ ] 652 - NEAReSt HUNDRED [ ]

Time: 10 seconds

6. [ ] $1\frac{1}{4} + 3\frac{1}{2}$ [ ]

7. [ ] Twice 7.3 [ ]

8. [ ] z = 4 calculate 4z − 7 [ ]

9. [ ] 8 times a number is 320. what is the Number [ ]

10. [ ]

WHAT time is in FIFty minutes.

---

11. [ ] THE Perimeter os a regular octagon is [ ] cm 72 cm What is the lenght os each side

12. [ ] 38% eqhavalent to in Decimal

13. [ ] imagine a cube, How MANy Vertices does it have? [ ]

14. [ ] write down the multiple of NINE between 100 and 110 [ ]

15. [ ] kg 2780 g to the nerest kg

Time: 15 seconds

16. [ ] what is the reminder when 67 is divided by 7

17. [ ] How mnch Smaller is 8.3 [ ] 12.4 than

18. £[ ] 4 PACKets of crisps cost £1.60 what will 7 Packets cost?

19. [ ] There are 3 angles on a straight line. Two of the angles 20 and 85° what is the third angle —

20. [ ] What is 18 multiplied by nine.

Total [ ]

page 15

Set
B

KEY STAGE 2
Levels 3–5

Test Paper 1

Maths

Test Paper 1 (calculator **not** allowed)

Test Paper 1 (calculator **not** allowed)

Instructions:

- find a quiet place where you can sit down and complete the test paper undisturbed
- make sure you have all the necessary equipment to complete the test paper
- read the questions carefully
- answer all the questions in this booklet
- go through and check your answers when you have finished the test paper

Time:

This test paper is **45 minutes** long.

Note to Parents:

Check how your child has done against the mark scheme in the Instructions, Answers and Mark Scheme Booklet.

Page	3	5	7	9	11	13	15	Max. Mark	**Actual Mark**
Score	....	....	....	....	....	....	....	40	....

First name ....

Last name ....

1 Write the missing numbers below.

a) $(6 \times 5) - \boxed{} = 13$

(1 mark)

b) $75 + \boxed{} = 140$

(1 mark)

2 The start of a football match is shown on the clock below.

The kick-off time is delayed by 20 minutes.

What time does the match start? $\boxed{}$

(1 mark)

3 Here is a parallelogram drawn on a graph.

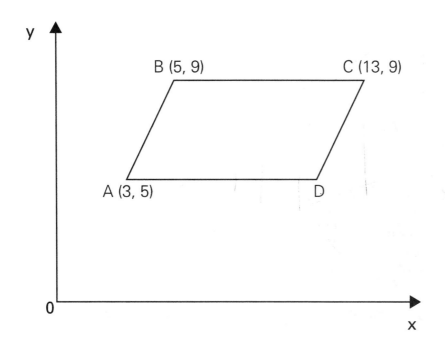

What are the coordinates of point D?

(☐ , ☐)

(1 mark) ☐
Q3

4 Complete the sequence below.

50 ☐ 100 125 ☐ 175 200

(1 mark) ☐
Q4

5 A shopkeeper kept a record of the different people that came into his shop on a Saturday. He put the results into a pie chart.

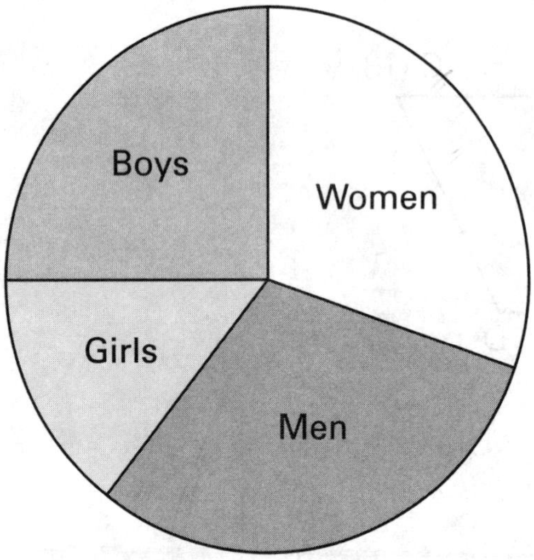

Total 120 people

a) Estimate the number of girls who entered the shop. ☐ *(1 mark)*

b) Did more male or female people enter the shop? Circle your answer.

MALE   FEMALE

Explain why you think this.

_____

_____

_____

_____

_____

_____ *(1 mark)*

6 The highest daytime temperatures in London, New York and Paris for a day in March are shown below.

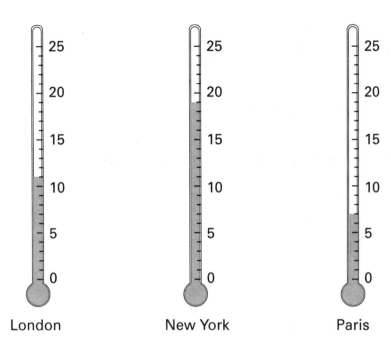

London   New York   Paris

How many degrees warmer was it in New York than Paris? ☐ °C

(1 mark)

Q6

7 Calculate   742 ÷ 14   ☐

Show your working. You may get a mark.

(2 marks)

Q7

Turn over

subtotal

8 Look at the four number cards.

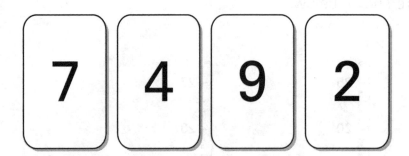

Choose three cards to make an odd number greater than 500.

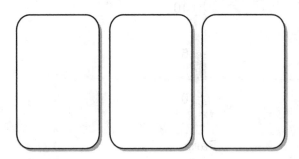

(1 mark)

Q8

9 Look at the diagram below. **Draw the line of symmetry of the shaded shape.**

You may use a mirror or tracing paper.

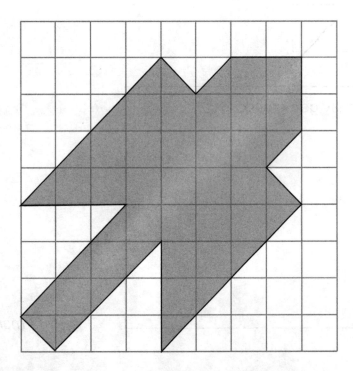

(1 mark)

Q9

10 Write in the missing digits.

| 2 | 9 | | + | 4 | | 7 | = | 7 | 8 | 4 |

(1 mark)

11 Look at this diagram.

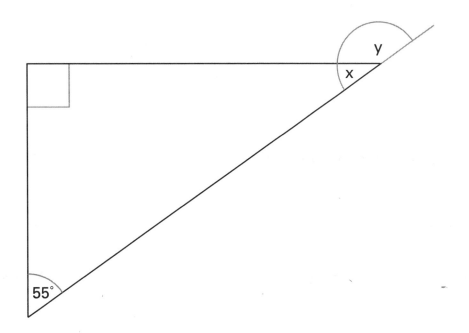

55°

Calculate angle x and then calculate angle y.

Do not use a protractor.

a) X = [   ]°

(1 mark)

b) y = [   ]°

(1 mark)

12

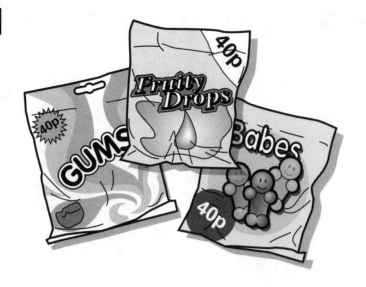

A bag of sweets weighs 120 grams and costs 40p.

a) **How much do five bags of sweets cost?**

(1 mark)

Sally spends £1.60 on sweets.

b) **What is the weight of Sally's sweets?**

(2 marks)

Show your working. You may get a mark.

13 This table shows the weights of four children.

Complete the table.

	grams	kilos
Amy	37 000	37
Alex		31.5
Ben	40 500	
Charlie		37.02

(2 marks)

Q13

14 Here is an equilateral triangle inside a rectangle.

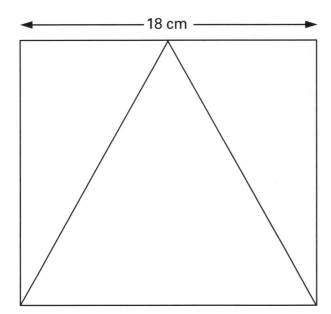

← 18 cm →

What is the perimeter of the equilateral triangle? ☐ cm *(1 mark)*

Q14

15 Circle the three numbers that divide by 6 with no remainder.

47	48	49
50	51	52
53	54	55
56	57	58
59	60	61
62	63	64

(1 mark)

Q15

16

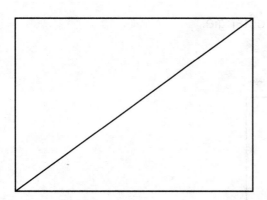

Measure accurately the length of the diagonal of this rectangle.

Give your answer in centimetres. [   ] cm   *(1 mark)*

Q16

17 Calculate $20.04 - 18.98 = $ ☐

(1 mark)

Q17

18 Calculate $\frac{3}{5}$ of $685 = $ ☐

(1 mark)

Q18

19 Draw the reflection of the shaded shape in the mirror line.

You may use a mirror or tracing paper.

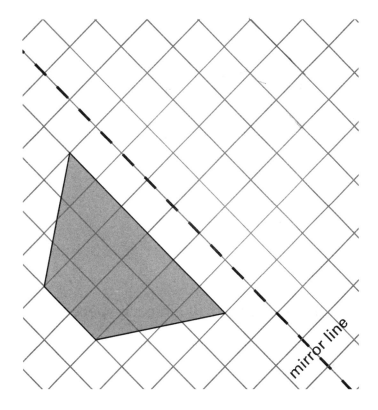

(1 mark)

Q19

20 Calculate $1107 - 211$ ☐

(1 mark)

Q20

21 Circle all the multiples of 7 in the list of numbers.

17   21   35   47   36   *(1 mark)*

22 Write each of the following numbers in the correct place on the Venn diagram below.

21   14   13

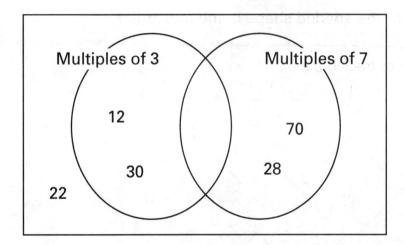

(2 marks)

23 Here is a sorting diagram for numbers.

Write a number greater than 20 but less than 100 in each space.

	even	square number
a multiple of 6		
a multiple of 8		

(2 marks)

24 Complete these fractions so that they are equivalent.

$$\frac{}{4} \qquad \frac{}{2} \qquad \frac{}{8} \qquad \frac{}{32}$$

(2 marks) Q24

25 There are 14 paint brushes in a box.

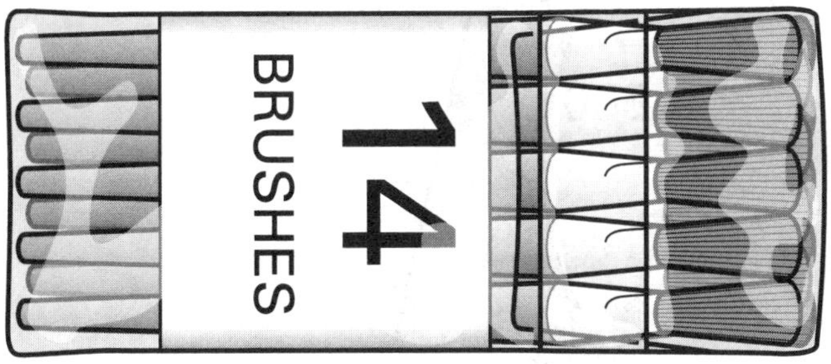

The school buys 21 boxes of brushes.

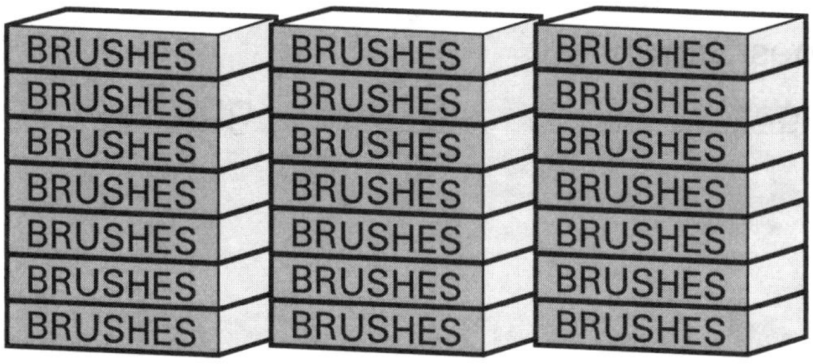

How many brushes does the school buy?

(2 marks) Q25

Show your working. You may get a mark.

Turn over

subtotal

26 Harry weighs some sugar. He weighs 475 grams of sugar.

a) Draw an arrow on the scale to show 475 grams.

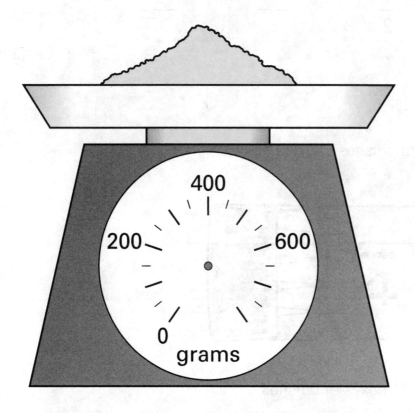

(1 mark)

b) How much more sugar does Sam need to get a total of 1 kg of sugar?

grams   *(1 mark)*

27 Here are five shapes on a square grid.

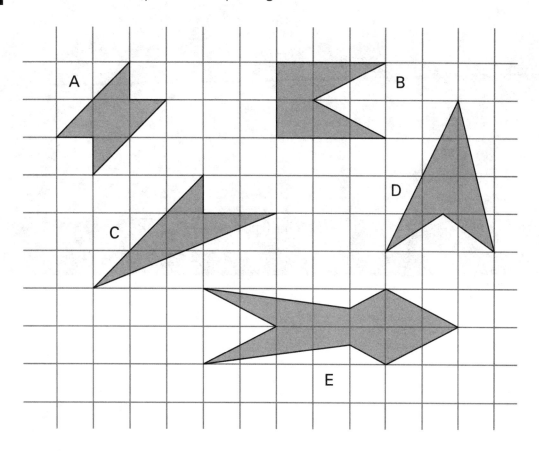

Write the letters of the two shapes which do not have a line of symmetry.

Shape ☐ and Shape ☐

(2 marks) ☐

END OF TEST

Set C

KEY STAGE 2
Levels 3–5

Test Paper 2

Maths

Test Paper 2 (calculator allowed)
& Mental Arithmetic Test

Test Paper 2 (calculator allowed)
& Mental Arithmetic Test

2+2

Instructions:

- find a quiet place where you can sit down and complete the test paper undisturbed
- make sure you have all the necessary equipment to complete the test paper
- read the questions carefully
- answer all the questions in this booklet
- go through and check your answers when you have finished the test paper

Time:

This test paper is **45 minutes** long.

Note to Parents:

Check how your child has done against the mark scheme in the Instructions, Answers and Mark Scheme Booklet.

Page	3	5	7	9	11	13	15	Max. Mark	**Actual** **Mark**
Score	....	....	....	....	....	....	....	40	....

Mental Arithmetic Test

Max. Mark	**Actual** **Mark**
20	....

First name ....

Last name ....

Letts

1 Complete the diagram below to make a shape that is **symmetrical** about the **mirror line**.

You may use a mirror or tracing paper.

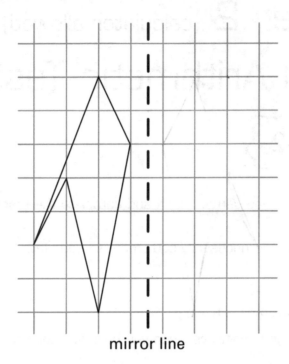

mirror line

(1 mark)

Q1

2 Circle the number that is closest to 115.

85   150   215   515   511   *(1 mark)*

Q2

3 Flower seeds are available in packs of 40 seeds and packs of 100 seeds.

Sally needs 960 seeds for a display in her garden.

There are only six packs of 100 seeds available in the shop.

What is the smallest number of packs Sally can buy from the shop to get 960 seeds?

Show your working. You may get a mark.

(2 marks)

Q3

4 The amount of rainfall was measured during last year.

Here is a chart showing the information recorded.

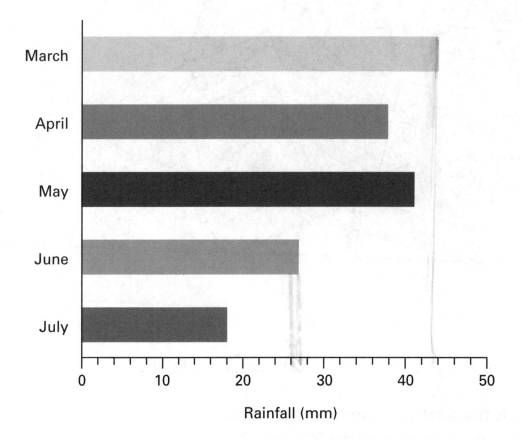

Rainfall (mm)

a) How much rainfall was there in **June**? ⬚ mm   *(1 mark)*   ☐
                                                                       Q4a

b) How much more rainfall was there in **March** than **July**? ⬚ mm

                                                              (1 mark)   ☐
                                                                          Q4b

5 Write in the missing numbers.

a) $279.3 = (39.9 \times$ ⬚ $)$ *(1 mark)*   ☐
                                                      Q5a

b) $980 - (85.9 \times 7.4) =$ ⬚   *(1 mark)*   ☐
                                                        Q5b

6 These are the prices of snacks at the school disco.

small soda	**50p**
large soda	**75p**
crisps	**35p**
chocolate bar	**40p**

Jack has **£3**; he wants to buy three large sodas, two chocolate bars and three bags of crisps.

How much **more** money does Jack need? £

Show your working. You may get a mark.

(2 marks)

Q6

Turn over

subtotal

7 A number sequence has the rule:

Take 6 away from the previous number, then add 18.

Complete the number sequence using this rule.

13 [ ] [ ] [ ]

(2 marks) [ ]

8 Here is a clock.

a) What time was it 50 minutes ago? [ ] *(1 mark)* [ ]

Here is another clock.

b) What time is it in 35 minutes? [ ] *(1 mark)*

[ ]

9   Calculate 30% of 390   ☐   *(1 mark)*   ☐

10   Here is a shape on a square grid.

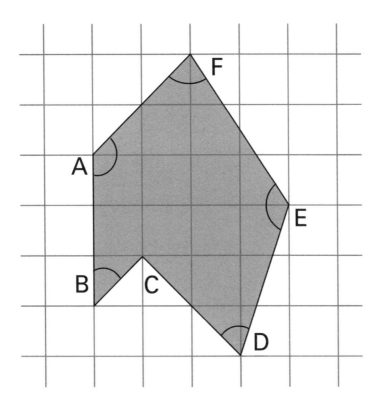

For each sentence, put a tick (✔) if it is true. Put a cross (✘) if it is untrue.

Line **CD** is parallel to line **EF**.   ☐

Line **BC** is parallel to line **AF**.   ☐

Angle **F** is a right angle.   ☐

Angle **E** is obtuse.   ☐   *(2 marks)*   ☐

11 Jack has three cans of fizzy drink.

He pours all three cans into a jug.

a) Draw the correct level on the jug below.

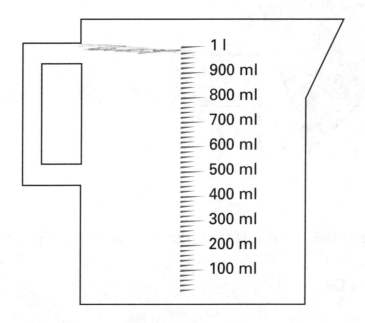

(1 mark)

Jack shares the fizzy drink between six children.

b) How much fizzy drink will they have each? ml   *(1 mark)*

12

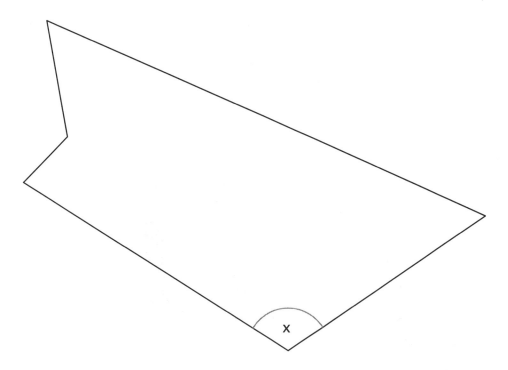

Measure angle x accurately.

Use an angle measurer (a protractor).

[   ] °

(1 mark)

13 Here is a diagram for sorting numbers.

Write one number in each section of the diagram.

	less than 200	more than 200
even number that divides by 7		
odd number that divides by 7		

(2 marks)

Turn over

14 Here is an equilateral triangle with four smaller equilateral triangles inside it.

The shaded triangle has a perimeter of 27 cm.

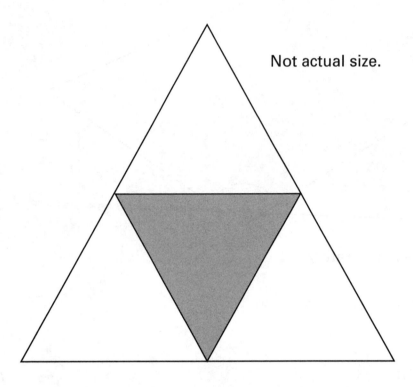

Not actual size.

What is the perimeter of the large equilateral triangle? ☐ cm

Show your working. You may get a mark.

(2 marks)

15 Write in the missing numbers.

a) $913 - \boxed{} = 471$

(1 mark)

b) $\boxed{} \times 89 = 356$

(1 mark)

16 Water was heated up during a science lesson.

The temperature was recorded and the time taken throughout the experiment. The results are shown on the graph below.

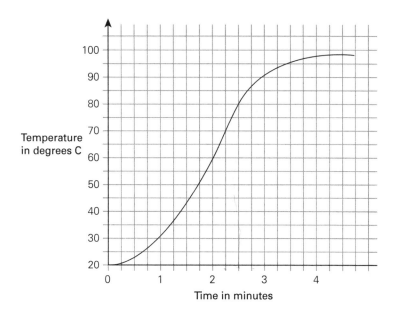

a) Read from the graph. How long does it take for the temperature to reach 80°C? $\boxed{}$ minutes *(1 mark)*

b) Use the graph to work out how many degrees the water heated up from one to three minutes. $\boxed{}$°C

(1 mark)

Turn over

17 Calculate $\frac{5}{8}$ of 576 ⬚

(1 mark)

Q17

18 Write in the missing numbers.

(⬚ × 9) ÷ 4 = 36

(1 mark)

Q18

19 Here are two regular octagons with shaded triangles inside them.

Under each octagon put a circle around the correct name of the shaded triangle.

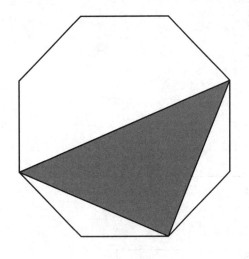 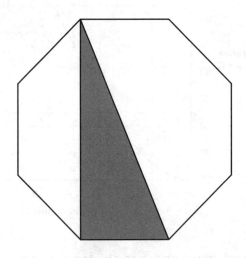

scalene   scalene

equilateral   equilateral

isosceles   isosceles   *(2 marks)*

Q19

20 Eighteen people go bowling together.

> **Adults £2.99 per game**
>
> **Children £1.99 per game**

There are six adults and twelve children.

a) How much does it cost altogether for one game? £ ☐

Show your working. You may get a mark.

(2 marks) ☐
Q20a

Drinks cost 55p each.

b) How many people had a drink if they spent £7.15? ☐ *(1 mark)* ☐
Q20b

21 Here is a regular pentagon.

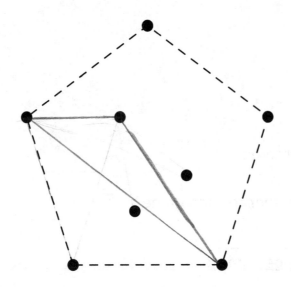

a) Join any three of the dots to make a scalene triangle.   *(1 mark)*

Here is a square.

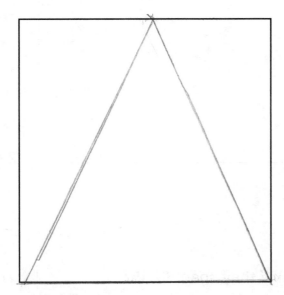

b) Draw an isosceles triangle inside the square. All corners of the triangle must touch the edge of the square.

Use a ruler.   *(1 mark)*

22 x, y and z each stand for a whole number.

x + y + z = 160

z is **three times** bigger than x.

y is **ten greater** than x.

Calculate the numbers x, y and z.

Show your working. You may get a mark.

X =

y =

z =

(3 marks)

END OF TEST

subtotal

Set C – Mental Arithmetic Test

The questions for this test are on page 14 of the Instructions, Answers and Mark Scheme Booklet.

Time: 5 seconds

1 [ ] [ ]

2 [ ] ml [ ]

3 [ ] [ ]

4 [ ] : [ ] [ ]

5 [ ] 56 [ ]

12 [ ] 300 [ ]

13 [ ] [ ]

14 [ ] 900 [ ]

15 [ ] mins [ ]

Time: 10 seconds

6 [ ] 80   470 [ ]

7 [ ] 64 [ ]

8 [ ] 370 [ ]

9 [ ] 800 [ ]

10 [ ] mins $10\frac{3}{4}$ hrs [ ]

11 [ ] m   128 m [ ]

Time: 15 seconds

16 [ ] 47   95 [ ]

17 [ ] 4.7 [ ]

18 £ [ ] £14   £8 [ ]

19 £ [ ] £1.08 [ ]

20 [ ] 90   70 [ ]

Total [ ]